POPPO'S
Memory Book
A Child's Guide to Remember and S.M.I.L.E. after Loss

Annie MacDonald, M.Ed.

Illustrated by Ashley MacNeil

authorHOUSE®

AuthorHouse™
1663 Liberty Drive
Bloomington, IN 47403
www.authorhouse.com
Phone: 1-800-839-8640

First published by AuthorHouse 12/13/2011

ISBN: 978-1-4670-7315-8 (e)
ISBN: 978-1-4670-7273-1 (sc)

Library of Congress Control Number: 2011919611

Printed in the United States of America

POPPO'S
Memory Book

ABOUT THE AUTHOR

Annie MacDonald, M.Ed., lives in New Hampshire with her husband. An elementary school counselor, Annie has worked with young children for over twenty five years. She is the author of the POPPO Books, a series inspired by the death of her graduate school professor. The series was created to help children who are coping with the failing health and death of a loved one move beyond their grief to feel happiness again.

For more information please visit www.mypoppo.org

The POPPO Books
What's up with Poppo?
Poppo's Half-Birthday Wish
Poppo's Very Best Trick
Bubbles for Poppo

ACKNOWLEDGEMENTS

Without the patience, love and support from my family and friends, *The Poppo Books* would not have been created. I am grateful to all who have shared this journey with me.

A special thanks to: Jim, Peter, Andy, Jenny, Ray, Donna, Tim, Steve, Gina, Nancy, Debbie, Pauline, Carlos, Cheri, Liz, Terrie, Janet, Lin, Jerry, Amy, Marie, Angie, Kary, Helena, David, Shelley, Kristie, Jeff, Jim H., Linda B., Linda M., Walter – TV-5, The Reading Lady – Karen, and to my friends at Fellowships of the Spirit in New York, and at Benjamin Franklin Elementary School in New Hampshire

Dr. Grace Lincoln - for your time, consultation, and curriculum expertise

And to Mom, Poppo and Bucko
Always smiling in my heart

POPPO'S Memory Book
A Child's Guide to Remember and S.M.I.L.E. after Loss

For families, teachers, counselors, and anyone
helping a child grieve the loss of a loved one

- Provides a healing model to help children deal with loss after death

- Offers a spiritual framework for children to understand the loss of a loved one

- Addresses loss after death honestly and directly, but remains comforting and hopeful

- Provides a way for children to identify and express their feelings through storytelling, creative arts, written and verbal self-expression, imagination, and conversation

- Creates a starting place for conversation with children

- Elicits the *tough* questions that arise when someone you love dies

- Incorporates the following key points through the use of the acronym S.M.I.L.E.

Share
Share your feelings with someone you trust.

Memories
Remembering keeps your loved one close.

Imagine
Use your imagination to create mind-magic.

Love
Love yourself and others too.

Enjoy
Enjoy your life in a new way.
Those we love never really die; they live in our hearts forever!

Why This Book Was Written

POPPO'S Memory Book - *A Child's Guide to Remember and S.M.I.L.E. after Loss* is not meant to be a traditional book on grief and loss. It is written as a companion guide for the four POPPO Books, a series created for children coping with the failing health and death of a loved one. This guide was written to accompany the final two books in the series, *Poppo's Very Best Trick* and *Bubbles for Poppo*.

Death is a difficult but natural part of life. As adults, our natural desire is to protect and shield children from the sorrow and pain that arises when loss occurs. Death is part of our life's journey. Through the death experience, we have an important opportunity to teach our children how to grieve. Our personal religious or cultural beliefs can be helpful to us, but these beliefs vary, as do the responses and explanations of death. The intention of this book is to offer a spiritual framework for children to understand death, while providing a tool to help children move beyond their grief and feel happiness again.

How To Use This Book

This self-paced guide was written to help children explore and express their many feelings, thoughts and worries related to the death of a loved one. The activities were created to teach children how to hold the relationship with their loved one in their hearts so that it will continue to be a source of comfort and love. It is best if you can find a quiet location, and allow for as much uninterrupted time as possible, in order to encourage a rich and meaningful experience. When it is a shared journey between the caregiver and the child, there will be time for reflection, and it will create the opportunity for question and dialogue.

Meet Jenny and Poppo!

When Jenny was little, she dressed in her favorite pink ballerina dress, and then Mommy and Daddy would take her to visit her Poppo. Every Sunday, Jenny and Poppo played together, until one day he was too sick to play. Her Poppo was sick for a very long time.

Poppo had a very, very, serious illness, and over time, the illness made it difficult for him to do the things he used to do before he got sick. He lived for a long time, but eventually, his sickness got worse and his body stopped living. Jenny felt very sad when her Poppo died.

Poppo was a wonderful grandfather and teacher. Before he died, he showed Jenny how to perform fun magic tricks, to blow really big bubbles, and to use her imagination to pretend and have fun. But when Poppo got sick, he also wanted to help Jenny understand and feel comfortable with death. He told her death was a natural part of life, and that everyone and every part of nature would eventually die. He explained to her that sometimes people can get very, very sick and die, even though they do not want to die. It just happens sometimes. Poppo did not want Jenny to feel worried or sad. He wanted to help her feel safe, and to know how much she was loved.

Jenny felt very confused by this. She told him how scared she felt, and then she asked him this very important question.

"What will I do without you?" I asked Poppo.

"What will I do without you?" I asked Poppo. I felt sad. I wanted my Poppo to live forever.
"I want you to be happy," Poppo told me.
"I want you to know I love you now and forever. I want you to always play and pretend and be my dancing little girl."

Poppo told Jenny that his body would someday die, but that he would continue to live in her heart. He also taught her not to be afraid of death, and to always remember the happiness and love they shared.

Even after her Poppo died, Jenny knew she would be safe, and that there were many people in her life who would always love and take care of her. She knew that the love she felt in her heart would never go away, even after her Poppo died.

After a long time, Jenny's grandfather died. Jenny cried with her Mommy and Daddy. She really missed him. But Jenny still felt a warm glow of love inside her heart, just like Poppo said she would.

Special Love

"Special love, like the love you shared with Poppo is something we have inside our hearts all our lives," Daddy explained to me. "It helps us to learn how to love ourselves and to love other people. It helps everyone to smile, just like you and Poppo always smiled."

How can you continue to love
someone whom you don't see
or hear or feel, the same way
you did before their death?

How can you find happiness
once again, and know that your
loved one is still very close?

Before Poppo died, he wanted to help Jenny understand the answers to these very important questions. He wanted her to know they would love each other forever. Poppo's lessons helped her to understand this. Jenny knew his body would eventually die, but it did not mean that their love would end. Love never dies. He would always be her Poppo, and that would never change!

The love that Poppo shared with Jenny was a love that she would have in her heart for all her life. And by remembering this love, Jenny learned to love herself and to love other people too. Her happiness helps others to smile, just like she and Poppo always smiled.

And now, just like Jenny, it is your turn to try and do the same. On the next few pages, follow along and practice all the ways that Jenny learned to smile after her Poppo died. Complete all the activities, share your feelings, and know that you are very special.

Remember! When you miss the
person who has died, the sadness
you feel is a BIG sign that you
have love in your heart.

Share your love with the world and S.M.I.L.E.

Share

Memories

Imagine

Love

Enjoy

My Loved One Has Died

Write the name of your loved one here.

Special Facts

My loved one was born on this date:_____

My loved one died on this date:_____

We loved to do this together:_____

_____

Our favorite place to be together:_____

_____

Places we went together:_____

_____

_____

What I remember most:_____

_____

_____

SHARE

Share your feelings with someone you trust.

Feeling Bubbles

When someone dies you may experience many feelings and every feeling you have is important. Sometimes your feelings may surprise you or you may have many different feelings at once. This can be confusing. Whatever you are feeling, express it through writing, drawing, or talking to someone you trust.

Color the bubbles that show how you felt when your loved one died. If the feeling you want to share is not shown, write the feeling word in one of the empty bubbles.

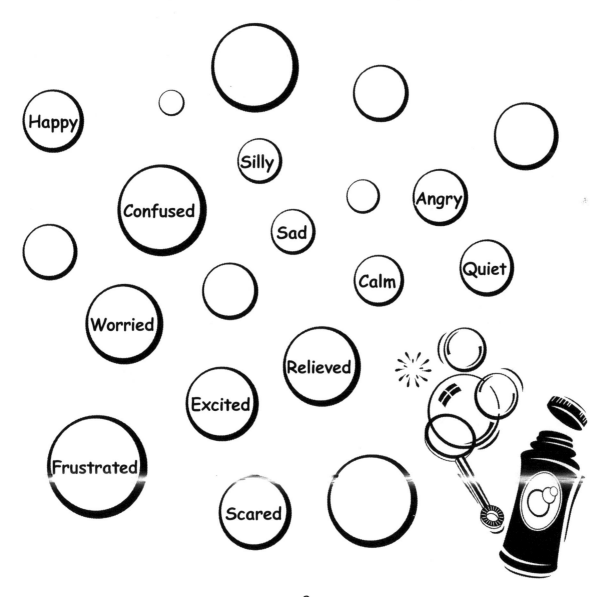

Happy · Silly · Confused · Sad · Angry · Calm · Quiet · Worried · Relieved · Excited · Frustrated · Scared

HOW I FELT
When My Loved One Died

Draw how your feelings showed on your face in the big bubble below.

I felt_____.

How I Feel
TODAY

Draw how your feelings show on your face now in the big bubble below.

Today I feel_____.

Questions and More Questions

Jenny asked her parents lots of questions! She wanted to understand all that she could about her grandfather and his illness. When she asked all her questions she was very brave.

YOU MAY HAVE QUESTIONS TOO!

What are they?
Write them on the next page.

"Poppo," I asked, "will you live forever?"

"What will I do without you?"

"So, Poppo's in Heaven?"

"How did Poppo die?"

"Who will do mind-magic with me?"

"So Poppo's spirit did not die?"

"Is Poppo with me now?"

"But I miss Poppo! Who will do mind-magic with me now?"

My Questions Are......

Talk To Someone You Trust

Sometimes, when I really miss Poppo, Mommy and Daddy encourage me to express my feelings. I ask them questions, and they try to help me understand.

It is important to find someone you trust and feel comfortable with to talk about your feelings. Can you think of people in your life you feel safe with, and you know love you very much? These are the people that would love to listen as you share all your feelings with them.

Jenny chose her parents, but there may be many others in your life that can be listeners and helpers for you. Sometimes relatives, teachers, or family friends can help you too.

Who can you talk to about your feelings?

_____

_____

_____

_____

_____

My Great
Listeners and Helpers

Letters To My Loved One

Dear Poppo,

I miss you and I love you very much.

Today I went to the park with mommy and daddy. We brought Aubrey to play too. We had lots of fun.

I remember your dog Max and I know he is with you. Do you play with him?

Give Max a hug for me. I miss you both.

I love you.

Jenny

With the help of her parents, Jenny found another way to express her feelings. She wrote many letters to her grandfather. Writing to her Poppo was another way Jenny kept her grandfather close in her heart.

Sometimes, Jenny shared her letters with her parents at night before she went to sleep. Other times, she wrote her thoughts when she was playing or watching television, or when she wanted to remember. She wanted Poppo to know just how important he was and would be forever. Expressing her feelings in this way helped Jenny to feel her Poppo with her, and to know he was still there, even if she couldn't see him anymore.

My Thoughts and Words

_____

_____

_____

_____

_____

_____

_____

_____

_____

_____

_____

_____

_____

_____

_____

_____

_____

_____

_____

_____

_____

_____

_____

_____

_____

_____

_____

_____

_____

_____

_____

_____

_____

_____

_____

_____

_____

_____

_____

_____

_____

_____

_____

_____

MEMORIES

Remembering keeps your loved one close.

Your memories help you to keep your loved ones close after they die. You can remember your loved ones as they were, and the many special things about them that make you smile.

When Poppo died, Jenny remembered Poppo's bright smile, his blue twinkling eyes, boat rides at the lake, dancing, performing magic tricks, blowing bubbles, and pretending and playing with her Poppo.

THERE ARE MANY WAYS TO REMEMBER.

You can look through photographs, share in special traditions, listen to stories, or simply spend time in places that remind you of your loved one. Writing letters, singing songs, dancing, or simply eating their favorite meal are ways to bring your loved one close. It doesn't matter how you remember, but simply that you do remember.

Sometimes, the memories you have can make you feel sad, angry, and even confused inside. That's okay. Don't be afraid to show these feelings too. All your feelings are important; share them with someone you trust. There are many people in your life who want to listen.

My Memories Are Special

Draw or attach pictures of you and your loved one.

23

Sharing Memories

Talk with your family and friends who knew your loved one. Ask them to share their memories with you. Sharing memories is a wonderful way to keep your loved one close in your heart.

Who did you ask?_____

Write about the special memory that was shared with you.

_____

_____

_____

_____

_____

Who did you ask?_____

Write about the special memory that was shared with you.

_____

_____

_____

_____

_____

Special Memories

Draw a picture of a special memory below.

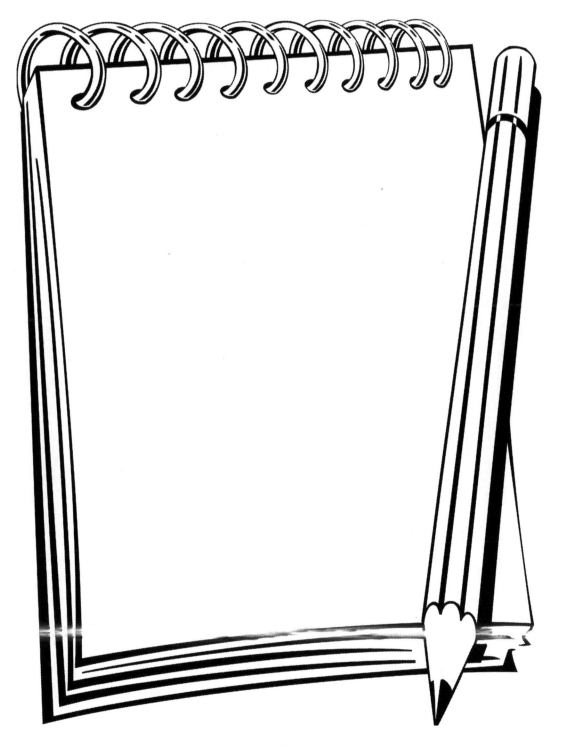

Special Ways To Remember

We walked along the path until we found the place where Poppo was buried. I could tell because there was no grass growing there. Mommy put a bouquet of flowers on the ground for Poppo.

When someone dies, you can do special things to help you remember. You may attend a funeral or memorial service, or do something fun like blowing bubbles or completing this memory book to help you to remember the person who has died. Thinking of special things to do can bring comfort, and help you to feel better when you are missing the physical presence of your loved one in your life.

After Poppo died, Jenny and her parents did special things to help them remember and honor him.

JENNY'S LIST OF SPECIAL WAYS TO REMEMBER

- I visit Poppo's grave at the cemetery.
- I share family stories about my Poppo.
- I continue to do the things I loved to do with Poppo (dancing in my pink ballerina dress, performing magic tricks, and pretending).
- I blow bubbles and send my love to Poppo.
- I write letters and draw pictures.
- I use my imagination to create, play and have fun.
- I try my best to feel happy and to share my happiness each day with my Poppo.

MY LIST OF SPECIAL WAYS TO REMEMBER

☆ ☆ ☆ ☆ ☆

1._____

_____

_____

2._____

_____

_____

3._____

_____

_____

4._____

_____

_____

Your family can help you create your own list of special ways to help you remember your loved one who has died. Write this list together. Then, on the next page, draw a picture that shows one of the special ways you have chosen to remember.

This Is One Way I Remember

IMAGINE

Use your imagination to
create mind-magic.

Mind-Magic Is Fun!

"My Poppo was always a super-duper pretender. Even when he was sick he could pretend to be anything he wanted to be. He called it mind-magic. Sometimes, he would make believe he could fly like a bird around the world. Sometimes, Poppo would make believe he was a superhero who could climb to the top of the highest mountain. He told me his imagination helped him to feel better. I could always tell Poppo felt better because he was always smiling."

When we use mind-magic, we are using our imagination. We are pretending, make-believing, wishing, dreaming, and most importantly we are having fun! Now it's your turn. On the next few pages, use your imagination and don't forget to have fun!

My Imagination Is Magical

Your imagination can help you to visit places you've never been, like a faraway island or distant land.

Where would you go?

_____

_____

What would you see?

_____

_____

Your imagination can help you to dream about things you wish you could do.

What do you wish you could do?

_____

_____

If you could have any super-power what would it be?

_____

_____

My Magical Imagination

Draw what you imagine!

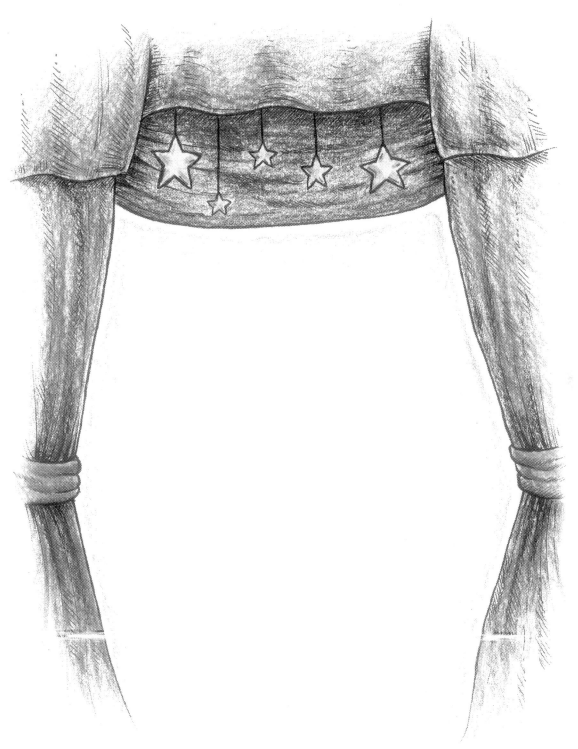

What Is Poppo's Very Best Trick?

You can use your imagination in another way too. Your imagination can help you to keep your loved one close in your heart after they die. Jenny learned this very important lesson from her grandfather.

"How will I know you are with me?" I asked. I did not want my Poppo to go anywhere.

"That's our very best trick," Poppo told me with a smile. "After I die, when you look into your heart you will always know I am with you. In your heart is where I will be smiling."

When Poppo got sick his body died, but his spirit did not die. Some people say that when a person dies their soul or spirit stays in the hearts of the people they love. After Poppo died, Jenny continued to feel his love in her heart. She could feel his spirit with her, keeping her company, just like he did when they could really be together.

Poppo wanted Jenny to know that he would always be her grandfather, and that he would always love her, even when she could no longer see him. He taught her how to keep him close, to feel his love, and to remember him with a smile in her heart whenever she felt sad.

My Mind-Magic!

Now it is your turn to create mind-magic! Close your eyes and imagine your loved one in your mind. Think of what it would be like if they were with you right now. Imagine you are still together. Feel your loved one in your heart, and know that they are with you in spirit and will always love you. Draw what you see or feel.

LOVE

Love yourself and others too.

Poppo taught Jenny many lessons, but the most important lesson she learned was about love. Jenny loved her grandfather very much. But he taught her how important it is to share that love with others. Poppo wanted Jenny to always feel love in her heart, to practice kindness, and to share her love with others. Jenny knew the best way to show kindness was to be respectful, to smile, and to have fun just like she did with her Poppo before he died.

Circle all the ways you show kindness.

I smile and say hello

I invite others to play

I take turns when I play a game

I use my manners

I listen when someone talks to me

I apologize

I help others when I can

I play fair

I give compliments to myself

I share my things

I am patient with myself

I try my best

I give compliments to others

I choose kind words

I know it's okay to make mistakes

I am patient with others

I forgive myself

I forgive others

Kindness Counts!

Jenny showed love and kindness to her parents in all that they did together. Whether it was decorating a cake, or helping with the household chores, Jenny tried her best. She showed kindness through her words and actions to her parents, siblings, teachers, and friends. Jenny wanted to share the love in her heart with everyone around her. It helped her to feel happy inside.

Write about a time you showed kindness to someone. Draw a picture on the next page.

_____

_____

_____

_____

How I Show Kindness

My Heart Is A Compass

It points me in the right direction, and it shows me how to feel love and to be happy.

When someone you love dies, your heart is what keeps you close to the person that you loved. You may not be able to see them, but you can feel the person in your heart. Your relationship with your loved one does not end. It continues on in a new way.

Our Time Together

Take some time now to think about all the things you did together before your loved one died. What do you remember most? Your special memories can help you to still feel close and remember just how important your loved one is to you.

Circle all the ways you spent your time together.

We read stories

We learned things

We went places together

We did activities

We listened to each other

We played games

We went for walks

We played outside

We watched TV

We loved each other

We went shopping

We fixed things

**Were there other ways you spent your time?
Write them here.**

_____

_____

_____

_____

_____

My Rainbow

When we love someone who has died, our heart builds a bridge filled with all the colors of the rainbow. Each color reminds us of all the ways we love; all our memories, experiences and feelings.

RED reminds Jenny of Poppo's bright smile
BLUE reminds Jenny of Poppo's twinkling blue eyes
YELLOW reminds Jenny of the lake and all her boat rides with Poppo
PINK reminds Jenny of her pink ballerina dress and dancing for Poppo

Jenny's rainbow was painted colors that reminded her of Poppo. Now, it's your turn. As you color the rainbow below, choose the colors that remind you of your loved one.

The Colors Of My Rainbow

Look at your rainbow. What colors did you choose? Can you share why these colors are special to you? Write your answer on the space next to the color word below.

RED_____

BLUE_____

YELLOW_____

GREEN_____

PURPLE_____

ORANGE_____

Did you add another color to your rainbow? Write it here.

_____

_____

ENJOY!

Enjoy your life in a new way.

> *"Now I know Poppo is with me all the time. I still can't see or hear him the way I used to, but I feel him in my heart. I can feel Poppo's soul inside me keeping me company, just like he did when we could really be together. I know Poppo loves me from Heaven, his soul tells me."*

THOSE WE LOVE NEVER REALLY DIE; THEY LIVE IN OUR HEARTS FOREVER!

Jenny did not forget her grandfather after he died. She understood that he was still her grandfather, and that he could be with her in spirit. Jenny learned to live her life with him in a new way. She kept him close to her heart by thinking of all their special times, and by doing the things that made her feel happy inside. She blew bubbles, danced in her pink ballerina dress, practiced mind-magic, performed magic tricks, asked lots of questions, shared her feelings, and completed a memory book like this one. She continued to love her Poppo, to think of him, and talk to him each and every day.

When you think about the person who died and remember all the love you shared, your love grows stronger and stronger. You can believe in your heart that your loved one is with you. And that will help you smile!

Do What Makes You Happy

Don't stop doing all those things you love to do just because your loved one has died. Your happiness is important. Your loved one will always be with you in your heart. That will never change. Invite your loved one to share in all you do and know that you always are loved!

One Thing I LOVE To Do!

Moving On

Moving on with your life after someone dies can seem difficult and scary. It is hard not to see and feel and touch your loved one the way you did before they died. That is why it is so important to practice all the ways that Poppo taught Jenny to keep him close. Moving on does not have to be scary. It can be a new adventure, one that you can continue to share with your loved one in a new way.

Share all your feelings with the people that love you. Whatever you are feeling, express it through writing, drawing, or talking to someone that you trust. And don't be afraid to ask questions. Everything you have to say is important!

Memories are also important! Look through old photographs, participate in special traditions, share stories, and spend time in the places that remind you of your loved one. It doesn't matter how you remember, simply that you do!

Imagine! Use mind-magic to keep your loved one close in your heart. Imagine your loved one is with you, keeping you company, just like you did when you could really be together. Feel your loved one's spirit close to you and loving you. Your love for each other will never die.

Love and show kindness to yourself and others in every way you can. Remember the love you shared with your loved one, and allow yourself to feel it in your heart now. Practice kindness by smiling, helping others, and by doing things that makes you feel happy inside.

AND DON'T FORGET TO...

Enjoy and live your life in a new way. Keep your loved one close through your memories, and by doing the things that help you feel happy. Imagine your loved one is still with you, and feel all the love in your heart. Find reasons to be grateful for each and every day and for all the good things that come your way.

Imagine your loved one is still with you!

Always Feel Gratitude
In Your Heart

And when you go to bed each night, remember all the things that happened that day. Then think about all the good things, and say "thank you." Saying thank you will help you to stay positive and happy.

What I am thankful for today.

_____

_____

_____

_____

_____

_____

_____

_____

_____

_____

_____

Five Ways I Remember

Share

I share my feelings with someone I trust.

Memories

I remember to keep my loved one close.

Imagine

I use my imagination to create mind-magic.

Love

I love myself and others too.

Enjoy

I enjoy my life in a new way.

SMILE

"In your heart is where I
will be smiling." POPPO